EDGE BOOKS™

SUPER TRIVIA COLLECTION

# THIS BOOK MIGHT MAKE YOU GAG

BY CONNIE COLWELL MILLER

A COLLECTION OF CRAZY GROSS TRIVIA

CAPSTONE PRESS
a capstone imprint

Edge Books are published by Capstone Press,
1710 Roe Crest Drive, North Mankato, Minnesota 56003.
www.capstonepub.com

Books published by Capstone Press are manufactured with paper
containing at least 10 percent post-consumer waste.

*Library of Congress Cataloging-in-Publication Data*
Miller, Connie Colwell, 1976–
    This book might make you gag : a collection of crazy, gross trivia / by Connie Colwell Miller.
    p. cm.—(Edge books. Super trivia collection.)
    Summary: "Describes a variety of gross trivia facts about bugs and animals, food, history, and
the human body"—Provided by publisher.
    Includes bibliographical references and index.
    ISBN 978-1-4296-7653-3 (library binding)
    1. Science—Miscellanea—Juvenile literature. 2. Curiosities and wonders—Juvenile literature.
I. Title. II. Series.
Q173.M642 2012
502'.07—dc23                                              2011028641

**Editorial Credits**

Aaron Sautter, editor; Alison Thiele, designer; Svetlana Zhurkin, media researcher;
    Laura Manthe, production specialist

**Photo Credits**

Alamy: Amazon-Images, 11 (top), Medical-on-Line, 26 (top), North Wind Picture Archives, 17
(middle right); Corbis: Catherine Karnow, 28–29, Ludovic Maisant, 13 (bottom); Dreamstime:
Fredweiss, 17 (middle left), Mathew Hayward, 4–5, Nina Schnapp, cover (bottom right), 10
(top), Photoeuphoria, 26 (bottom), roblan, 23 (top); Getty Images: David McLain, 14 (bottom),
DEA/A. Dagli Orti, 20 (top); iStockphoto: Hector Joseph Lumang, 15 (bottom), Hippo Studio,
12 (middle), Michael Courtney, 24 (bottom); Library of Congress, 19 (top); Mary Evans Picture
Library, 16, 20 (bottom); Newscom: akg-images, 21 (top); akg-images/Jorgen Sorges, 18 (top);
Photolibrary: Brandon Cole, 7 (bottom); Shutterstock: Adrian Niederhauser, 12 (bottom), Andre
Adams, cover (bottom left), 1 (bottom left), Anna Subbotina, 1 (top), Chardchanin, 17 (top),
Croato, 9, discpicture, 25 (top), Fernando Cortes (background), cover and throughout, Four
Oaks, 7 (top), ilFede, 22, Jan Kowalski, 25 (bottom), lineartestpilot, 3 (bottom), 17 (bottom), 27
(bottom), lsantilli, cover (top), 1 (bottom right), mikeledray, 8 (bottom), Olena Pivnenko, 14 (top),
Olga Donskaya, 27 (top), Paul Cowan, 13 (top), Sam DCruz, 10 (bottom), Sergey Mikhaylov,
6 (bottom), SFerdon, 18 (bottom), Studio 37, 19 (bottom), SvitalskyBros, 11 (bottom), Tony
Oshlick, 24 (top), Tootles, 23 (bottom), Tribalium, 21 (bottom), Vava Vladimir Jovanovic, 15 (top),
Vinicius Tupinamba, 8 (middle), wonderisland, cover (bottom middle); Visuals Unlimited: David
Phillips, 23 (middle); Wikipedia: Zylornian, 6 (middle)

Printed in the United States of America in Stevens Point, Wisconsin.

102011      006404WZS12

# TABLE OF CONTENTS

Introduction: GROSSER THAN GROSS........ 4

Chapter 1: THE CRUDEST CRITTERS .......... 6

Chapter 2: DISGUSTING DISHES ............. 12

Chapter 3: VILE TIMES ...................... 16

Chapter 4: YOU DISGUST ME! .................. 22

Glossary ..............................30

Read More ............................31

Internet Sites .......................31

Index................................32

# GROSSER THAN GROSS

Some animals fling their poop. Some people use maggots to make cheese. People once even used pigeon droppings as hair dye. No matter where you look, people and animals do disgusting, gross things.

Most gross things are gross for a reason. Gross smells and tastes warn others to keep away. And it's usually best to avoid things that make our stomachs turn. However, we live in a strange world filled with all sorts of weird and wacky things. People from different parts of the world have different ideas of what's gross. If you think something is totally disgusting, someone somewhere might think it's beautiful or delicious.

Read on to learn about some of the grossest things on planet Earth. But be warned—you're sure to gag before you're done!

# Chapter 1

# THE CRUDEST CRITTERS

Some critters seem to always be trying to gross us out. Some use poop in strange ways. Others eat animals from the inside out. These animals usually have good reasons for doing such gross things. But it may make you barf when you read about it!

When it feels threatened, the horned lizard squirts blood from its eyes. This gross action doesn't hurt the lizard. But it does send enemies running.

Hippopotamuses have a disgusting way of showing who's boss. These big brutes swing their tails to swat balls of poop all over. The smelly act is their way of marking out territory and telling others to back off.

Screwworm flies lay their eggs in the open wounds of warm-blooded animals. Many insects feed on the dead tissues of a wounded animal. But screwworm larvae eat living tissue. These maggots can actually eat an animal alive.

The kids will love this!

Dung beetles love poop! Some of these little bugs roll up tiny balls of poop for their future mates. Female beetles then lay their eggs inside the balls. The baby beetles eat the nutritious poop when they hatch.

The revolting hagfish has at least two disgusting behaviors. First, when threatened it produces big gobs of slime as protection against predators. It also has a gross way of eating. It grabs hold of a dead or dying fish and then bores a hole into its prey. It may also slither inside the fish's body through its mouth, gills, or rear end. Then the hagfish eats its victim from the inside out!

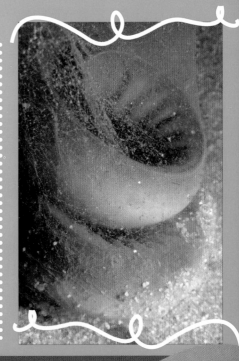

larva—an insect at the stage of development between an egg and an adult

prey—an animal hunted by another animal for food

The pharaoh ant has a unique diet. It will eat regular ant foods like sugar and bread. But the tiny ant prefers meat and fat. It's been known to sneak into hospitals to dine on medical garbage. It seems to especially like blood and pus found in used bandages.

Earthworms have a disgusting way of eating. They "barf" their throats out of their mouths to grab their food. When they have a mouthful, the earthworms pull their throats back into their bodies.

Are they gone yet?

Opossums sometimes use a unique defense when they feel threatened. They fall over and poop so enemies think they're dead. It usually works. After all, who would want to eat a filthy, dead opossum?

Flies don't have teeth to chew their food like people. They vomit their digestive juices onto it instead. The fly barf turns the food into a soupy mess. Then the fly can suck the food up through its strawlike mouth parts.

## A Pain in the Rear

Pinworms are tiny worms that can live inside your digestive system. Female worms wiggle down to your rear end to lay their eggs. At the same time, they release a chemical that causes intense itching. But scratching down there isn't a good idea. Pinworm eggs can get stuck beneath your fingernails. You could pass pinworms onto other people. People who have pinworms may even see the tiny critters come out in the toilet or in their underwear.

One of a face fly's favorite foods is snot! It loves the mucus that oozes out of a large animal's mouth, nose, and eyes. That's disgusting enough. But face flies also tend to spread eye diseases as they buzz from animal to animal.

Do you know why vultures are bald? Because it's not nearly as messy to shove a bald head into the body of a dead animal. Feathers would trap bits of rotting meat and blood on the vulture's head. The bloody mess could cause disease.

Let's eat!

Pass the ketchup!

The human botfly attaches its eggs to a mosquito or other blood-sucking insect. When the mosquito bites someone, the eggs drop off and hatch. Then the larvae crawl into the hole in the skin left behind by the mosquito. Inside the skin, the maggot feeds and grows until it's big enough to wiggle out and become a botfly. Botfly maggots often cause painful sores in a person's skin. They're usually not deadly—but they are super gross!

May the stinkiest dude win! Male lemurs have an odd way of finding a mate. They rub their bushy tails on smelly **glands** on their arms and chests. Then they wave their stinky tails at each other in a "stink fight." The lemur that stinks the worst usually wins the girl, and the loser runs away.

**gland**—an organ in the body that produces natural chemicals

# Chapter 2
# DISGUSTING DISHES

The saying goes, "You are what you eat." And from bugs to brains, it seems there's nothing some people won't eat.

Fried or roasted grasshoppers are a treat in some parts of the world. People in Thailand buy the crunchy critters by the bagful. They munch them like peanuts or popcorn!

In the Philippines some people dine on the brains of live monkeys! The animals are first given rice wine to make them drunk. Once they pass out, their skulls are cut open to have their brains scooped out. The practice is illegal. But some people continue to do it in the belief that it cures certain health problems.

People from Scotland sometimes eat haggis. The sausage-like meat is made from animal organs like sheep hearts, livers, and lungs. The meat is mixed with oatmeal, onions, and spices. Then it's stuffed into a casing of beef *intestines* to be cooked.

Vampires think blood is delicious. But they're not alone. Blood pudding, also called black pudding or blood sausage, is served in many parts of the world. The sausage is made with *congealed* animal blood mixed with oatmeal and spices. The blood for most pudding comes from pigs or sheep. Fans of blood pudding say it tastes like any other kind of sausage.

*intestine*—a long tube that carries and digests food

*congeal*—to change from a liquid to a solid

People sometimes eat the tongues of cows, which are very high in fat. Some cow tongue is even sold with the taste buds still attached!

In Sardinia people make a type of cheese called casu marzu. When the cheese is ready, flies are allowed to lay their eggs in it. When the eggs hatch, the maggots begin feeding on the cheese. Their digestive juices begin to decompose it. The process makes the cheese very soft, and it creates a flavor some people love. Eating half-digested cheese is gross enough. But that's not the worst part. The maggots tend to jump around a lot when you start cutting into the cheese!

Delicious!

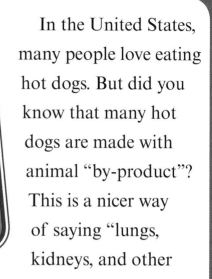

In the United States, many people love eating hot dogs. But did you know that many hot dogs are made with animal "by-product"? This is a nicer way of saying "lungs, kidneys, and other parts." Many people don't realize they're eating ground-up animal parts they'd normally avoid.

People in several countries eat octopus. But in Japan and South Korea, it's considered a real treat. Living octopuses are sliced up so people can swallow the still wiggling tentacles.

# Chapter 3
# VILE TIMES

Hundreds of years ago, people were dirtier, sicker, and generally grosser than today. People didn't know much about germs back then. They didn't take a lot of care to keep things clean or use safe medical methods. These are just a few of the disgusting things people have done throughout history.

People didn't always have toilets available. Instead they pooped and peed in pots they kept in their homes. Each day they emptied the pots by dumping them out a window. They'd shout a warning to anyone passing by on the street below. The waste was then swept into the city's sewers.

Look out below!

Ever wonder why people shake with their right hands? Long ago people usually used their left hands to wipe themselves after going to the bathroom. So people used their "clean" right hands to greet others. Even today, greeting someone with your left hand is considered an insult in some countries!

Ancient Romans used some really gross stuff to color their hair. To make their hair lighter, ladies smeared pigeon poop and pee on it. To darken their hair, they used mashed-up dead leeches.

During the Civil War (1861–1865), soldiers used bat poop, or guano, to make gunpowder. The guano was used to produce nitrates. Nitrates are an important ingredient in gunpowder and explosives.

From about AD 400–1700, many people believed a surgery called trepanation was a cure for headaches. The treatment involved drilling a hole into the patient's skull. The hole supposedly released pressure on the brain, which would relieve the headaches.

Skulls of more ancient people have also been found with trepanation holes in them. It's thought that they believed the holes allowed evil spirits to escape a person's body.

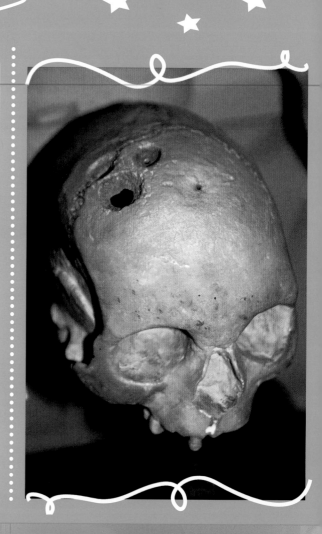

Belching after a good meal is considered good manners in some cultures. A big burp lets the cook know the food was satisfying. Tell that to your mom the next time you let one slip after dinner!

culture—a people's way of life, customs, and traditions

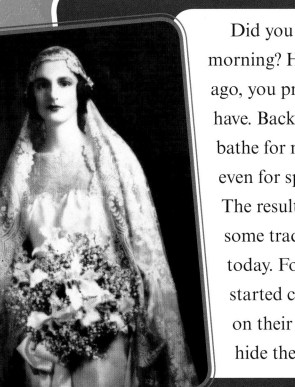

Did you have a shower this morning? Hundreds of years ago, you probably wouldn't have. Back then, people didn't bathe for months at a time, even for special occasions. The resulting body odor led to some traditions we still follow today. For example, brides started carrying flowers on their wedding days to hide their smelly body odor.

Most people know the ancient Egyptians made mummies. But did you know they pulled the dead person's brain through the nose with a hook? They didn't think the brain did much, so they simply threw it out. Meanwhile, most of the body's other organs were preserved in special jars.

The black plague was a horrible disease that was greatly feared in the Middle Ages (about AD 400–1500). The plague first infected a person's lymph nodes. Victims developed huge lumps called **buboes** in their groin and armpits. The disease also caused high fevers, severe headaches, muscle pain, and blood vomiting. Tens of millions of people died from the disease in the Middle Ages.

Leprosy was once a disease feared by many people. The disease causes large, revolting sores on people's skin. Left untreated, leprosy can cause people to lose feeling in their hands, arms, and legs. Eventually these body parts become useless. It was once thought the disease caused body parts to decay and fall off. But this was found to be untrue.

*bubo*—a swelling of a lymph gland

Long ago, people once believed that diseases were caused by too much blood in the body. Doctors often practiced bloodletting. They sliced open patients' arms and allowed their blood to pour out. The doctors thought less blood would return the patients to good health. However, this practice usually just made patients weaker and sicker. Sometimes they even died from the process.

The first public toilets were simply big pits in the ground. Everybody would do their duty in the same hole. To cover up the stink, they just threw some dirt on top of it. Unfortunately, the dirt didn't work too well. Most people found these public "privies" simply by following their nose.

# Chapter 4
# YOU DISGUST ME!

Animals can be awfully disgusting. But there's something that can be considered even grosser—you! With boogers and barf and poop and pee, your own body is pretty gross too.

Everyone does it!

People's bodies are like factories. They are always working to keep people healthy and energetic. But like all factories, the human body is constantly producing waste. The average adult produces about 1/3 pound (0.15 kilogram) of poop and 1.5 quarts (1.4 liters) of pee every day.

Did you know that dried-up earwax is always falling out of your ears? If you use earphones a lot, you probably have a lot of wax built up in there. Earphones can prevent the wax from drying up and falling out the way it should. So unplug and let the wax fly!

Your body constantly sheds old skin cells and makes new ones. Day and night, billions of dead skin cells fall off people and float around their homes. Dead skin cells actually make up most of the dust in your home.

Some people have tried drinking their own pee to avoid dehydration. But it's not a good idea. Your pee is full of salts and waste products that your body is trying to get rid of.

Your body is basically a big snot-making machine. Your **mucous membranes** constantly make snot that traps germs, dust, and other icky stuff. Although snot is useful, it's still gross. On average, people swallow about 1 quart (0.9 liter) of snot every day!

A build-up of gas in your intestines causes farting. The gas comes from the breakdown of foods in your body. The average person passes about 0.5 quart (0.47 l) of gas a day. Farts stink because of a gas called hydrogen sulfide that is created as food is digested. Farts stink more if people eat foods that are rich in sulfur, such as beans or cabbage.

**mucous membrane**—a soft tissue in the body that creates mucus

Eww, nasty!

Sweating helps keep your body cool. If that's the case, then your feet must be the coolest! Together your feet can produce 1 cup (240 milliliters) of sweat every day. People's feet are almost always covered by socks and shoes, which keep them warm. The sweat from feet can't evaporate and becomes trapped. No wonder a person's gym socks reek!

Everyone gets sweaty armpits sometimes. But did you know the sweatiest parts of the body may be the palms of your hands? Your hands have more sweat glands than any other part of the body. Good thing we wash our hands as much as we do!

You can't see them, but most people have tiny bugs called demodex mites living in their eyelashes. These little critters like to eat dead skin cells and the fluids from your eyes.

Almost got it!

Picking your nose isn't just gross—it can also spread germs. Your nose produces plenty of snot that traps germs. When the snot dries out, it makes the boogers that you're tempted to pick out. But the germs are still there. You can spread those germs by digging in there and then touching other things. Be sure to blow your nose with a tissue instead.

Zzzzzzz...

Ever wonder why your breath stinks in the morning? When you sleep, your spit doesn't flow much. Any bits of food left in your mouth don't get washed away. Rotting food just sits there all night, causing that horrible morning breath!

You've probably heard of a heart transplant. But have you heard about someone getting a poop transplant? The procedure is used for people suffering from severe digestive problems. Doctors first take a poop sample from a family member and process it. Then it's placed in the patient's stomach through a tube in the nose. The foreign poop contains healthy **bacteria** that help balance the patient's digestive system.

**bacteria**—one-celled, microscopic organisms that exist all around you and inside you

# OUR DISGUSTING WORLD

Gross stuff can be found anywhere you look. It might lurk under a rock. It might be something an animal does. It may even be inside of you! But if you think something is disgusting, someone somewhere probably thinks differently.

It's OK to be totally grossed out by something you think is disgusting. Just remember—gross stuff has its place in the world too!

# GLOSSARY

**bacteria** (bak-TEER-ee-uh)—one-celled, microscopic organisms that exist all around you and inside you; many bacteria are useful, but some cause disease

**bubo** (BYU-bo)—a swelling of a lymph node, often in the groin

**congeal** (kuhn-JEEL)—to change from a liquid to a solid

**culture** (KUHL-chuhr)—a people's way of life, ideas, customs, and traditions

**gland** (GLAND)—an organ in the body that produces natural chemicals

**intestine** (in-TESS-tin)—a long tube that carries and digests food and stores waste products

**larva** (LAR-vuh)—an insect at the stage of development between an egg and an adult

**mucous membrane** (MYOO-kuhss MEM-brayn)—a soft tissue in the body that creates mucus

**prey** (PRAY)—an animal hunted by another animal for food

# READ MORE

**National Geographic Kids.** *Weird But True! 300 Outrageous Facts.* Washington, D.C.: National Geographic, 2011.

**Scholastic, Inc.** *Ripley's Believe It or Not! Special Edition 2011.* New York: Scholastic, 2011.

**Yomtov, Nel**. *The Grimy, Gross, Unusual History of the Toilet.* Unusual Histories. Mankato, Minn.: Capstone Press, 2012.

# INTERNET SITES

FactHound offers a safe, fun way to find Internet sites related to this book. All of the sites on FactHound have been researched by our staff.

Here's all you do:

Visit *www.facthound.com*

Type in this code: 9781429676533

Super-cool stuff!

Check out projects, games and lots more at
**www.capstonekids.com**

# INDEX

animals
    botflies, 11
    defenses, 4, 6, 7, 8
    dung beetles, 7
    earthworms, 8
    flies, 9, 10
    hagfish, 7
    hippopotamuses, 6
    horned lizards, 6
    insect eggs, 7, 9, 11, 14
    leeches, 17
    lemurs, 11
    opossums, 8
    pharaoh ants, 8
    pigeons, 4, 17
    pinworms, 9
    poop, 4, 6, 7, 8, 17
    screwworms, 7
    slime, 7
    snot, 10
    vultures, 10

blood, 6, 8, 10, 13, 21

foods
    blood pudding, 13
    casu marzu, 14
    cow tongues, 14
    grasshoppers, 12
    haggis, 13
    hot dogs, 15
    monkey brains, 12
    octopuses, 15

history
    bathing, 19
    black plague, 20
    bloodletting, 21
    burping, 18
    chamber pots, 16
    gunpowder, 17
    hair coloring, 4, 17
    leprosy, 20
    mummies, 19
    shaking hands, 17
    toilets, 21
    trepanation, 18

human body
    armpits, 20, 25
    boogers, 22, 26
    demodex mites, 26
    earwax, 23
    eyelashes, 26
    farting, 24
    morning breath, 27
    pee, 16, 22, 23
    poop, 16, 22
    poop transplants, 27
    skin, 11, 20, 23, 26
    snot, 24, 26
    sweating, 25

maggots, 4, 7, 11, 14
meat, 8, 10, 13